Croque-Anglais 3

Suzanne Fournier
Charles Côté

CROQUE-ANGLAIS 3

TRÉCARRÉ
QUEBECOR MEDIA

Catalogage avant publication de la Bibliothèque nationale du Canada

Fournier, Suzanne

Croque-anglais:

Pour les francophones étudiant l'anglais, langue seconde, au niveau primaire.
Sommaire: 3. Cahier d'activités d'anglais pour les enfants de 8 et 9 ans – 4. Cahier d'activités d'anglais pour les enfants de 9 et 10 ans

ISBN 2-89568-188-0

1. Anglais (Langue) - Problèmes et exercices - Ouvrages pour la jeunesse. 2. Anglais (Langue) - Manuel pour francophones - Ouvrages pour la jeunesse. 3. Anglais (Langue) - Vocabulaire - Problèmes et exercices - Ouvrages pour la jeunesse. J. Côté, Charles, 1967- . II. Titre.

PE1129.F7P68 2003   428.2'441'076   C2003-941223-7

Les Éditions du Trécarré remercient Catherine Laberge et Adrienne Fournier-Sirois pour leur précieuse collaboration.
Illustrations : Christine Battuz
Conception graphique et mise en pages : Cyclone design communications

© 2003 Éditions du Trécarré, division de Éditions Quebecor Média inc.

Tous droits réservés. Sauf pour de courtes citations dans une critique de journal ou de magazine, il est interdit de reproduire ou d'utiliser cet ouvrage, sous quelque forme que ce soit, par des moyens mécaniques, électroniques ou autres, connus présentement ou qui seraient inventés, y compris la xérographie, la photocopie ou l'enregistrement, de même que les systèmes informatiques.

Nous reconnaissons l'aide financière du gouvernement du Canada par l'entremise du Programme d'aide au développement de l'industrie de l'édition (PADIÉ) pour nos activités d'édition; du Conseil des Arts du Canada; de la SODEC; du gouvernement du Québec par l'entremise du Programme de crédit d'impôt pour l'édition de livres (gestion SODEC).

ISBN 2-89568-188-0

Dépôt légal 2003
Bibliothèque nationale du Québec

Imprimé au Canada

Éditions du Trécarré, division de Éditions Quebecor Média inc.
7, chemin Bates
Outremont (Québec) Canada
H4V 4V7

1 2 3 4 5 07 06 05 04 03

Mot aux parents

Chers parents,

Voici enfin la collection *Croque-Anglais*. Inspiré par le programme du ministère de l'Éducation, ce cahier d'activités permettra à votre enfant de s'initier à l'anglais ou d'approfondir ses connaissances de la langue de Shakespeare tout en s'amusant. Vous serez aussi appelés à participer en guidant votre enfant à travers les pages de ce livre et en répondant à ses interrogations ou aux petits sondages qu'il devra compléter. Encouragez-le à poser des questions, à être curieux et à persister dans ses efforts pour comprendre et utiliser l'anglais avec fierté.

Suivez les péripéties de Croque-Mots et de son nouvel ami Crocfun. Ils vous feront vivre de bons moments tout en explorant vocabulaire et notions de grammaire d'une manière ludique.

Have fun with Crocfun and your child

Suzanne Fournier et Charles Côté

Table of contents

Getting Started

Meet Mister Alpha

Mister Alpha's alphabet code

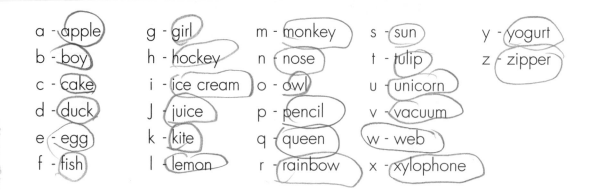

a - apple   g - girl   m - monkey   s - sun   y - yogurt
b - boy   h - hockey   n - nose   t - tulip   z - zipper
c - cake   i - ice cream   o - owl   u - unicorn
d - duck   J - juice   p - pencil   v - vacuum
e - egg   k - kite   q - queen   w - web
f - fish   l - lemon   r - rainbow   x - xylophone

Now we use the code. Write the words.

A apple	B boy	C cake	D duck	E egg	F fish
G girl	H hockey	I ice cream	J Juice	K kite	L lemon
M monkey	N nose	O owl	P pencil	Q queen	R rainbow
S sun	T tulip	U unicorn	V vacuum	W web	X xylophone
Y yogurt	Z zipper				

Match me if you can!

Draw a line between the first letter and the picture.

Letters   Pictures

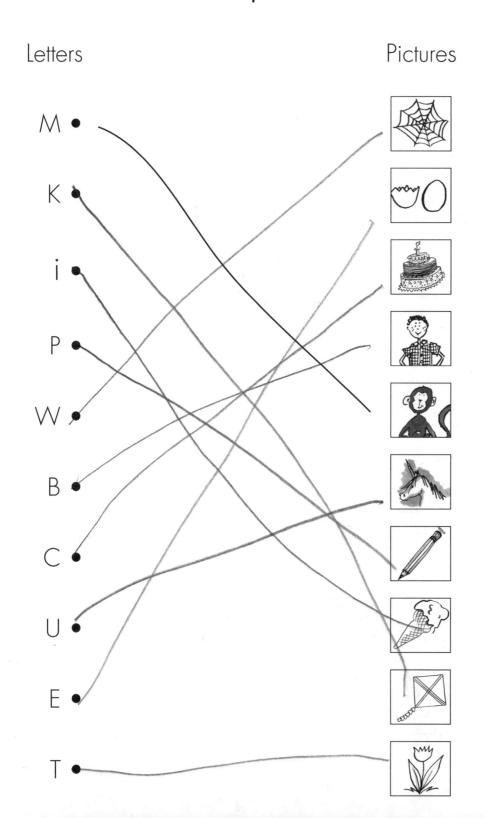

Mixed-up letters

1. Put the letters in order. Use Mister Alpha's code.

A. hfis _f i s h_   F. ckud _d u c k_

B. cohkey _h o c k e y_   G. neque _q u e e n_

C. snu _s u n_   H. ekac _c a k e_

D. wlo _o w l_   I. elppa _a p p l e_

E. lgri _g i r l_   J. oyurtg _y o g u r t_

2. Complete the message. Write the first letter of each word.

_c h a r l e s_   _p l a y s_

_t h e_

_x y l e p h o n e_

What do you think?

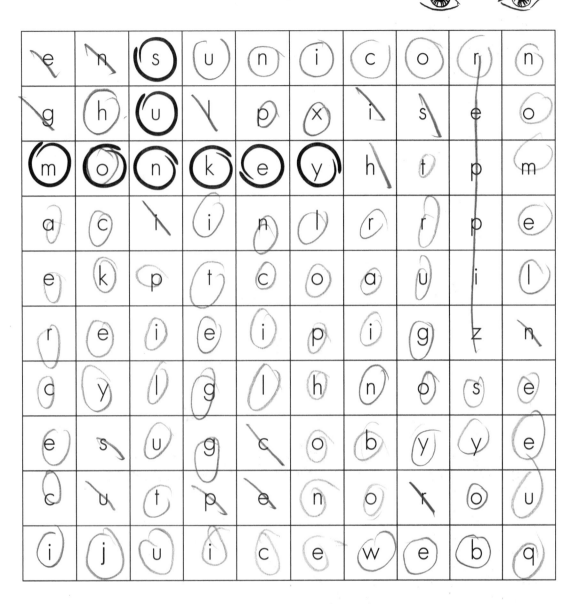

e	n	s	u	n	i	c	o	r	n
g	h	u	l	p	x	i	s	e	o
m	o	n	k	e	y	h	t	p	m
a	c	i	i	n	l	r	r	p	e
e	k	p	t	c	o	a	u	i	l
r	e	i	e	i	p	i	g	z	h
d	y	l	g	l	h	n	o	s	e
e	s	u	g	c	o	b	y	y	e
c	u	t	p	e	n	o	r	o	u
i	j	u	i	c	e	w	e	b	q

Find these words in the puzzle

☐ Boy	☐ Kite	☐ Queen	☐ Web
☐ Egg	☐ Lemon	☐ Rainbow	☐ Xylophone
☐ Hockey	☑ Monkey	☑ Sun	☐ Yogurt
☐ Ice cream	☐ Nose	☐ Tulip	☑ Zipper
☐ Juice	☐ Pencil	☐ Unicorn	

Mystery : _english is super_ !

Vowels and consonants

In English, the vowels are:
A, E, I, O, U, Y

The consonants are: B, C, D, F,
G, H, J, K, L, M, N, P, Q, R,
S, T, V, W, X, Z

There is no É, È, Ê, Î, Ô, Ë, Ï

Underline the <u>vowels</u> and circle the consonants

1. The monkey and the owl have funny eyes.

2. The tulip is pink.

3. The girl and the boy play hockey.

4. The sun and the lemon are yellow.

5. The queen eats ice cream.

14

You are the artist

Draw ...  Don't look ✗ ✗ at page 10

A web	An apple	An owl
A nose	A girl	Ice cream
A cake	Yogurt	A boy

Give it a go young Picasso

Now you choose

Draw  and write 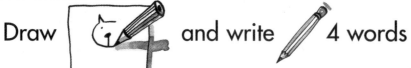 4 words

Example:

Cake

Add colours

Apple

Ice cream

egg

Nose

16

Numbers

Croque-Mots learns numbers

1 one   **2** two   **3** three   **4** four

5 five   **6** six   **7** seven   **8** eight

9 nine   **10** ten   **11** eleven   **12** twelve

Put the letters in order

1. neo   <u>one</u>

2. inne <u>nine</u>

3. vesen <u>seven</u>

4. lwteev <u>twelve</u>

5. tne <u>ten</u>

6. ghiet <u>eight</u>

7. rofu <u>four</u>

8. levene <u>eleven</u>

9. eterh <u>three</u>

10. wot <u>two</u>

11. ivef <u>five</u>

12. xis <u>six</u>

Draw a line

Draw a line between the number and the word.

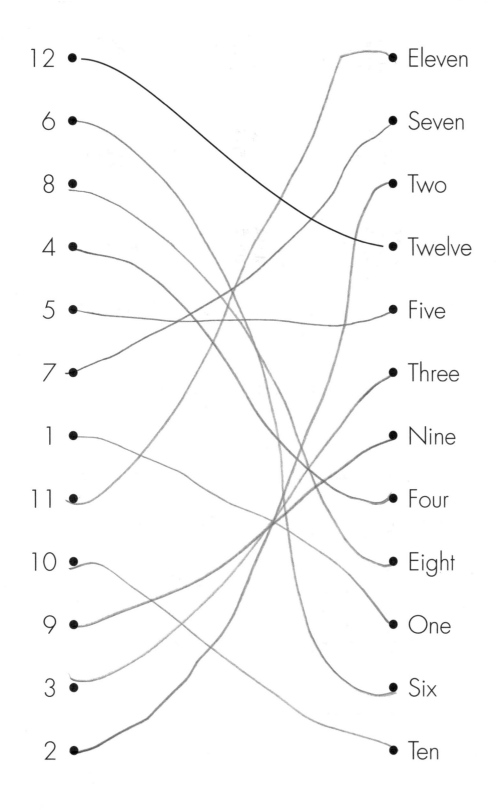

12

6

8

4

5

7

1

11

10

9

3

2

Eleven

Seven

Two

Twelve

Five

Three

Nine

Four

Eight

One

Six

Ten

Hidden numbers

Use Mister Alpha's code on page 10.

1. <u>T</u> <u>w</u> <u>e</u> <u>l</u> <u>v</u> <u>e</u>

2. <u>s</u> <u>i</u> <u>x</u>

3. <u>t</u> <u>w</u> <u>m</u>

4. <u>w</u> <u>i</u> <u>g</u> <u>h</u> <u>t</u>

5. <u>s</u> <u>w</u> <u>v</u> <u>w</u> <u>n</u>

6. <u>w</u> <u>l</u> <u>w</u> <u>v</u> <u>w</u> <u>n</u>

7. <u>f</u> <u>i</u> <u>v</u> <u>e</u>

8. <u>f</u> <u>o</u> <u>a</u> <u>r</u>

9. <u>n</u> <u>i</u> <u>n</u> <u>e</u>

10. <u>o</u> <u>n</u> <u>e</u>

Mathematics in English

0 = zero   Let's add! + + +

Write the correct number in letters.

1. five
    + two
    s e v e n

2. six
    + six
    twelve

3. five
    + four
    nine

4. two
    + two
    four

5. seven
    + one
    eight

6. eleven
   + zero
   eleven

7. zero
    eight
    + three
    eleven

8. three
    five
    + four
    twelve

9. zero
    six
    + four
    ten

10. four
     two
     + three
     nine

11. five
     three
     + two
     ten

12. one
     seven
     + two
     ten

21

Let's subtract!

Draw 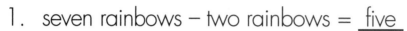 your answers. Check Mister Alpha's code.

1. seven rainbows – two rainbows = <u>five</u>

2. twelve kites – six kites = 6

6 Kites

3. five queens – four queens = 1

1 queen

4. eight girls – six girls = 2

2 girls

5. ten tulips – nine tulips = 1

1 tulip

6. four pencils – zero pencils = 4

4 pencils

The biggest fish

Choose the correct math symbol.
Your choices: >, <, or =

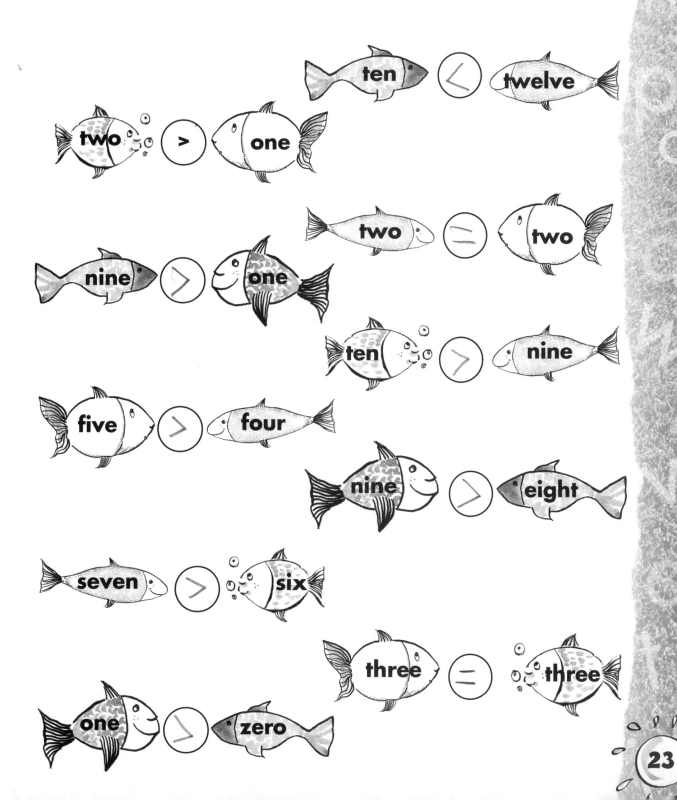

Let's multiply!

Croque-Mots x 1 = 1 Croque-Mots

Spell the answers.

1. two x two = four
2. ze ro x nine = zero
3. 1 ♡0 x 5 ♡0 = fire eggs
4. one x one = one
5. two x four = 8
6. 5 🌷 x ten 🌷 = ten __ __ l i __ __
7. one x two = two
8. seven x one = 7
9. three ☀ x 2 ☀ = six s __ n s
10. three x two = six
11. one x eleven = eleven
12. eleven ⬦ x one ⬦ = 11 __ i __ __ s
13. four x one = __ __ __ __
14. four x __ __ __ = eight
15. six x tw __ = tw __ __ __ __
16. five x two = __ __ __
17. two x __ __ __ __ = t __ n
18. one 🍋 x 0 🍋 = __ __ __ __ __ l __ m __ __ __
19. two x __ __ __ __ __ = six
20. zero x e __ __ ven = __ __ __ __

Find the place

Find 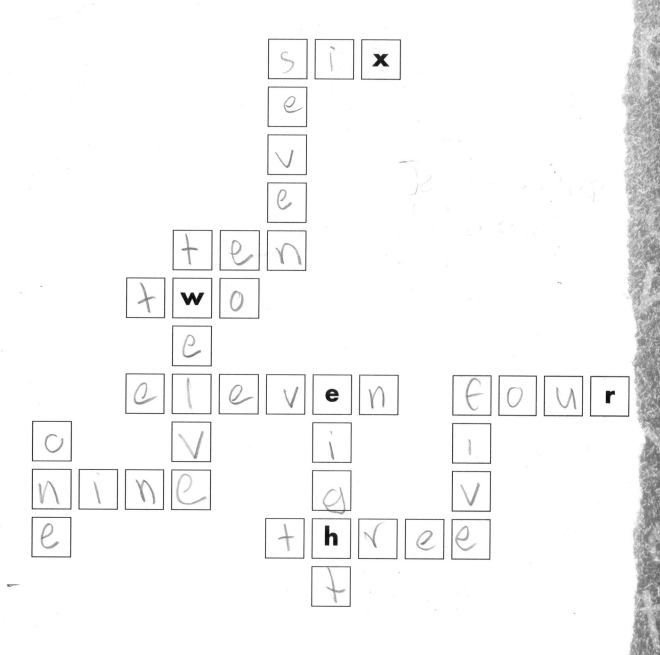 the correct place for numbers 1 to 12

		s	i	**x**						

(crossword puzzle)

```
            s  i  x
            e
            v
            e
      t  e  n
      t  w  o
         e
   e  l  e  v  e  n        f  o  u  r
o        v        i        l
n  i  n  e        g        v
e              t  h  r  e  e
                  t
```

25

Art, letters and numbers

Read   and draw

12 Draw twelve suns 	5 Draw five boys 
1 Draw one owl 	3 Draw three tulips 
6 Draw six zippers 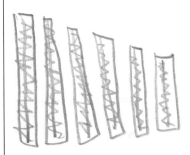	8 Draw eight kites 

More numbers

13 thirteen   **14** fourteen

15 fifteen

16 sixteen   **17** seventeen

18 eighteen

19 nineteen   **20** twenty

Complete the series:

1. two, three, _____four_____, five
2. sixteen, _____seventeen_____, eighteen, nineteen
3. five, _____six_____, _____seven_____, eight, nine
4. twenty, _____twentyone_____, eighteen, seventeen
5. two, four, six, _____eight nine_____, ten
6. twelve, fourteen, sixteen, _____seventeen_____
7. ten, _____eleven_____, eight, _____nine_____, six
8. thirteen, _____fourteen_____, fifteen, _____sixteen_____
9. five, _____four_____, _____three_____, _____two_____, one
10. eleven, _____twelve_____, fifteen, _____sixteen_____

Backpack knick-knacks!

Look 👁 👁 in the backpack and count!

1. I see ___six___ suns.

2. I see ___five___ tulips.

3. I see ___two___ girls.

4. I see ___two___ cakes.

5. I see ___one___ owl.

6. I see ___fifteen___ eggs.

7. I see ___five___ noses.

8. I see ___five___ pencils.

9. I see ___three___ boys.

10. I see ___sixteen___ lemons.

11. I see ___three___ kites.

12. I see ___one___ fish.

13. I see ___four___ xylophones.

14. I see ___one___ rainbow.

Which is which?

Circle (A) B C   the correct word.

1 =	on, own, (one) off
2 =	to, (two,) too, the
3 =	(three,) tea, tree, ten
4 =	for, from, (four,) floor
5 =	file, fifth, (five,) fly
6 =	sock, (six,) sick, stick
7 =	several, set, (seven,) sun
8 =	ate, (eight,) eat, egg
9 =	night, none, nose, (nine)
10 =	tell, twin, (ten,) tall
11 =	even, (eleven,) evening, elves
12 =	twenty, twin, ten, (twelve)
13 =	three, thirty, (thirteen)
14 =	four, (fourteen,) fifteen
15 =	fifth, five, (fifteen)
16 =	(sixteen,) six, seven
17 =	seven, (seventeen,) six
18 =	nineteen, fourteen, (eighteen)
19 =	eighteen, seventeen, (nineteen)
20 =	two, (twenty,) twelve

Croque-Mots wants to know...

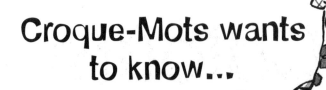

My lucky number is eleven!
What is your lucky number?

My lucky number is __100__ .

Now draw your lucky number.
Use colours!

What is your telephone number?

S-P-E-L-L your number: (514) 481 7585

Colours

Croque-Mots learns colours

bleu = blue   vert = green   gris = grey

brun = brown   jaune = yellow   rose = pink

rouge = red   noir = black   mauve = purple

blanc = white   beige = beige

Is this possible? Check ✔ "Yes" or "No"

	Yes	No			Yes	No
1. A blue elephant	☐	☐	6. A black duck	☐	☑
2. An orange orange	☑	☐	7. A purple lemon	☐	☑
3. A red heart	☑	☐	8. A beige apple	☐	☑
4. A yellow star	☑	☐	9. Pink yogurt	☑	☐
5. A green sun	☐	☑	10. A white egg	☑	☐

Make your own colour chart

Now colour these big pencils. Choose the correct colour.

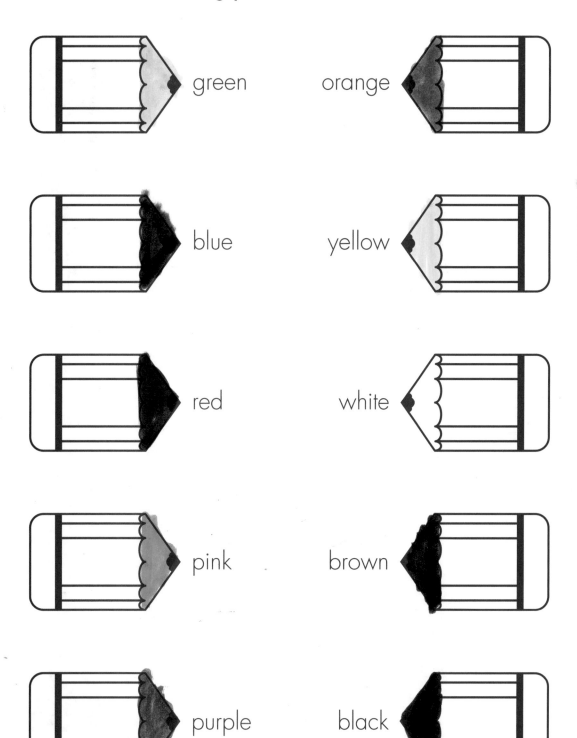

green   orange

blue   yellow

red   white

pink   brown

purple   black

Find colours

Use Mister Alpha's code to find 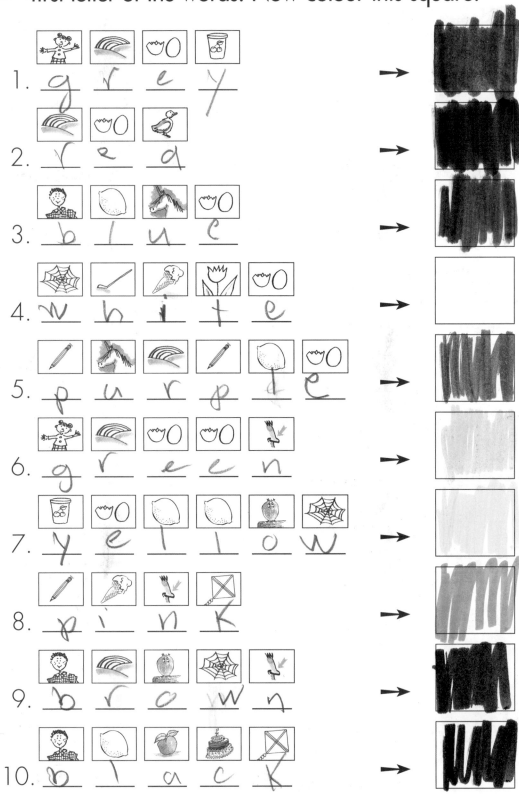 colours. Write the first letter of the words. Now colour this square.

1. g r e y   →

2. r e d   →

3. b l u e   →

4. w h i t e   →

5. p u r p l e   →

6. g r e e n   →

7. y e l l o w   →

8. p i n k   →

9. b r o w n   →

10. b l a c k   →

Cool colours

Follow the lines and colour the squares.

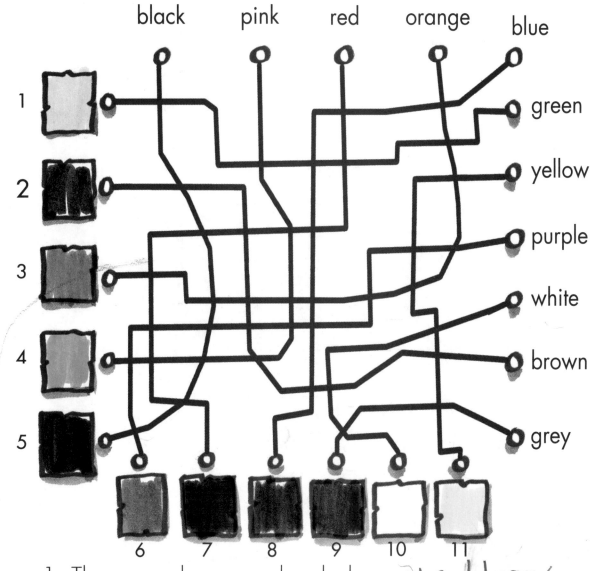

black   pink   red   orange   blue

green

yellow

purple

white

brown

grey

1. The sun, a lemon and a duck are _yellow_

2. An apple, a heart and a strawberry are _red_

3. A monkey, a hockey stick and a violin are _brown_

4. An egg, a unicorn and vanilla yogurt are _white_

5. A rainbow is _red, yellow, purple, orange, gre_ **35**
blea

Croque-Mots wants to know...

My favourite colour is green!
What is yours? _____

1. Colour this rectangle using your favourite colour!

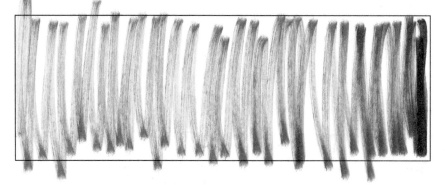

2. Now draw 3 objects that are your favourite colour
(example: an apple is red, a pig is pink).

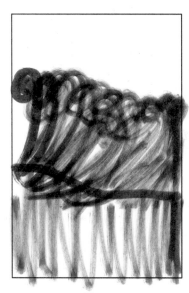 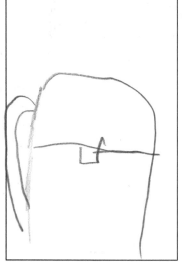 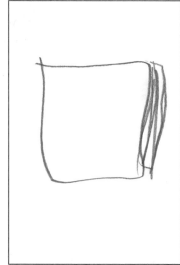

It is a __sea__   It is a __scool bag__   It is a __book__

Colouring fun

Colour this picture. Use this colour code.

eight = blue   sixteen = green

three = brown   twenty = yellow

eleven = red   thirteen = black

twelve = grey   nineteen = pink

fifteen = orange

Shape-up

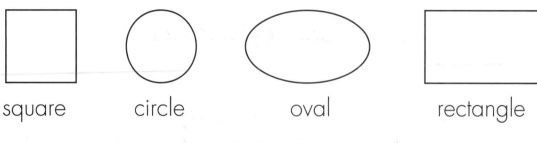

square   circle   oval   rectangle

triangle   heart   star

What shapes can you see  ?

1. A ball is a _circle_

2. A chocolate bar is a _rectangle_

3. This house has a _square_ and a _triangle_

4. This car has a _square_, a _rectangle_ and two _circle_.

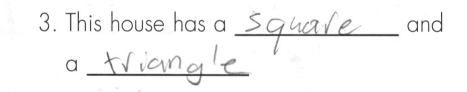

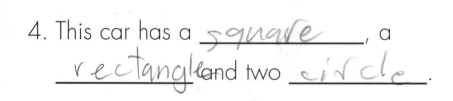

5. This elephant has two _triangle_, two _circle_ and five _rectangle_

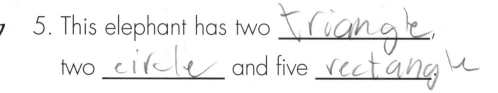

Be an artist

Can you draw objects? Use ...

Two circles

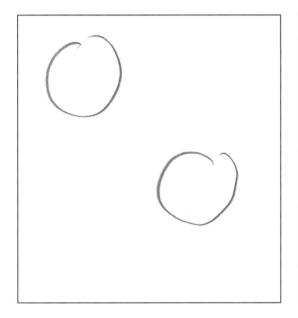

Four squares

One rectangle and
two stars

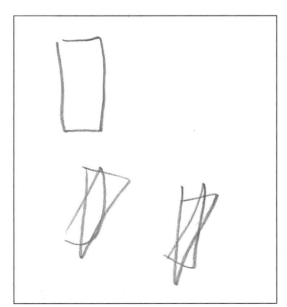

Three circles, four triangles
and one heart

Croque-Mots loves art

1. Draw a rectangle

2. Add a triangle

3. Add 2 triangles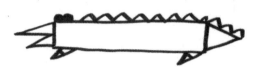

4. Add 2 half circles

5. Add 13 small triangles.
   You must colour the eyes.

Now it's your turn to draw a crocodile

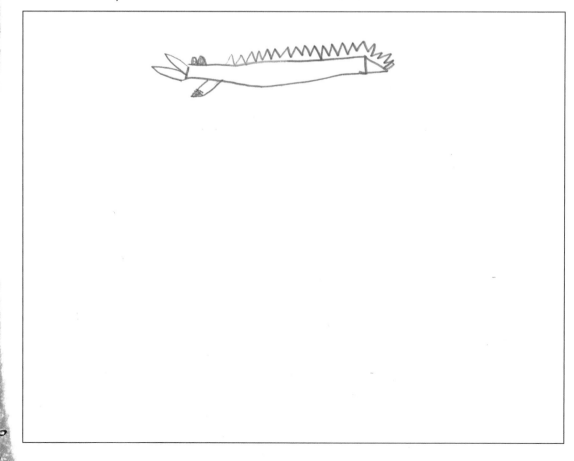

A dinosauro-shapus colourex

How many...

A. squares in this dinosaur? _six_

B. grey rectangles? _five_

C. grey circles? _five_

D. grey triangles? _tree_

E. stars? _tree_

F. hearts? _one_   H. white circles? _seven_

G. white rectangles? _twenyonl_   white triangles? _twenty_

Are you puzzled?

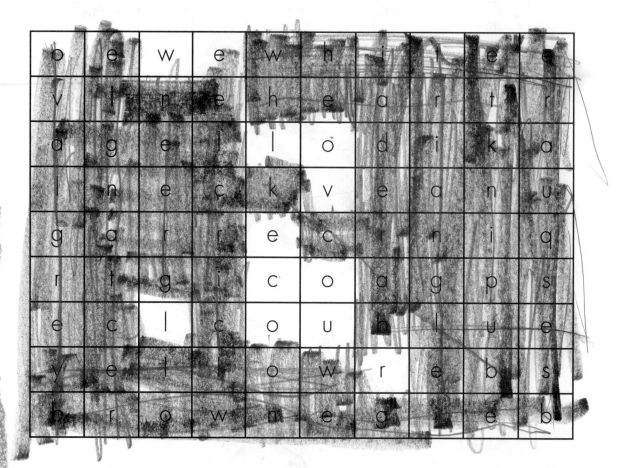

Circle the words in the puzzle.

Beige   Black   Blue
Brown   Green   Grey
Heart   Oval   Pink
Rectangle   Red   Square
Triangle   White   Yellow
Circle

Twette col Yours

Write the message here:
we

W e   l o v e   c o u l o u r s

Croque-Mots meets Crocfun

First meeting

Say hello!

Before lunch
"Avant-midi"
is **morning**
in English

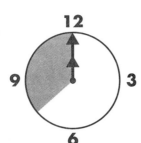

Before 12:00 or noon

After lunch
"Après-midi"
is **afternoon**
in English

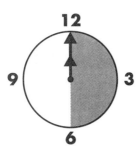

After 12:00 or noon

After supper
"Soirée"
is **evening**
in English

After 6:00 PM

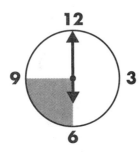

Before you go to bed
"Nuit" is **night**
in English

I lost my tongue

Complete the conversations. Write the words.
Look at "First meeting" on page 44
and "Say Hello" on page 45.

1. 3:00 PM or 3 o'clock

Good _Afternoon_

2. 9:00 PM or 9 o'clock

Good _night_ !

3. 11:00 AM

Good _Morning_!
I a_m_
f_i_n_e_ !

Good _Morning_
How a_r_e_
y_o_u_?

4. 7:00 PM

Good _evening_!
My _name_ _is_
Crocfun!

Good _evening_!
What's your
n_a_m_e_?

Halloween

Special occasions

October 31 is a special occasion for children. It is ...

HALLOWEEN

Halloween is during a season called **Fall** or **Autumn**. On this special occasion, children wear nice costumes and go door to door to collect candies and money ($) for Unicef. Happy Halloween!

Write your name. Draw big letters like **this**!

What costume?

The costume department

Look at the costumes, read the list and write the correct letter.

1. ⓘ
2. Ⓔ
3. Ⓒ
4. Ⓛ
5. Ⓖ
6. Ⓗ
7. Ⓓ
8. Ⓜ
9. Ⓐ
10. Ⓚ
11. Ⓕ
12. Ⓑ
13. Ⓙ

A. witch
B. bat
C. clown
D. pirate
E. cat
F. spider
G. skeleton
H. fairy
I. ghost
J. scarecrow
K. vampire
L. monster
M. ballerina

Riddles

Find the answers

1. What is white and goes **Boo Boo Boo?**

    g   h   o   s   t

2. Where do skeletons live?

    g   B   A   v   e   y   A   r   D

3. Who rides a broom?

    W   i   t   c   h

4. Who has a red 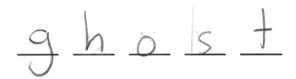 ?

    c   l   o   w   n

5. What goes "meow meow"?

    b   a   t

6. Who lives in a garden or a field?

    s   c   A   r   e   c   r   o   w

51

What is the mystery word?

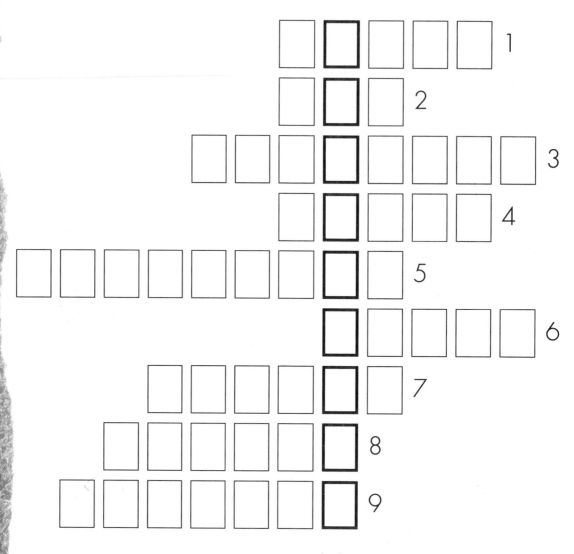

1. It is white, says "booo"
2. _ _ _ man
3. Lives in a graveyard
4. He has a big red nose
5. ♥ gardens
6. She wears a big black hat

7. Insect with 8 legs:
_ _ _ _ _ _ _
8. Man with a patch on his eye
9. Big, round and orange

The mystery word is celebrated on October 31.
Write it here.

_ _ _ _ _ _ _ _ _

Are you afraid?

Crocfun! Are you afraid of ghosts?

Oh yes, Croque-Mots!

afraid = avoir peur

What are you afraid of ... ?

Make a list of things you are afraid of ...
Draw the pictures.

A little (-)	A lot (+)
bat	witch
spider	Monster BOO

Jack-o'-lanterns

Did you know Croque-Mots, that a jack-o'-lantern is a pumpkin?

No!

It is a carved pumpkin.

A little bit, yes!

Like a sculpture?

This is a jack-o'-lantern

1. How many eyes does it have? <u>Ariel</u>

2. How many teeth does it have? <u>Ariel</u>

Halloween decorations

Some jack-o'-lanterns look **happy** …

Some jack-o'-lanterns look **mean** or **dangerous** …

I like those jack-o'-lanterns!

I am afraid of those jack-o'-lanterns!

Draw a jack-o'-lantern. Use colours! Have fun. Is it happy or mean?

Decisions

Draw yourself in a vampire costume	Draw yourself in a witch costume

56

Getting ready for October 31

I am trick or treating with my friend Crocfun. I am wearing a vampire costume.

And you? You are trick or treating with _____

You are wearing a _____ costume

Draw your Halloween costume. Use colours!

Colours for Halloween

In French, I say " Je porte un chapeau **noir**".
In English, I place the colour "black" **before** the
noun "hat". I say : "I am wearing a **black** hat".

colour before

Describe your Halloween costume.

I am wearing _____ boots or shoes.
                colour

I am wearing a _____ hat or cap.
                  colour

I am _____ _____ pants or dress.
              colour

I am wearing a _____ _____ .

(draw the accessory)

I __ ___ __ _____ _____ .

(draw the accessory)

58

Misplaced colours

What do you see 👁 👁 ?

A. An <u>orange</u>   <u>jack-o'-lantern</u>
        colour   noun

B. A _ _ _ _ _ _ _ _
         colour   noun

C. Two _ _ _ _ _ _ _ _ _ _ s
              colour   noun

D. One _ _ _ n _ s _
               colour   noun

Write in the correct order

1. hat one purple: <u>one</u> _____ _____
                         quantity   colour   noun

2. white skeleton a: _____ _____ _____
                            quantity   colour   noun

3. a cat brown: _____ _____ _____
                       quantity   colour   noun

4. pink a ballerina: _____ _____ _____
                            quantity   colour   noun

5. pirates two black and white: _____

6. black spiders eight: _____

7. brown three scarecrows: _____

8. monster green one: _____

59

Trick or treating in my neighbourhood

On October 31, I trick or treat on my street, Ocean Street, on River Street and on Lake Avenue. What about you? Where do you trick or treat? Name the streets. I trick or treat on _____

_____

_____

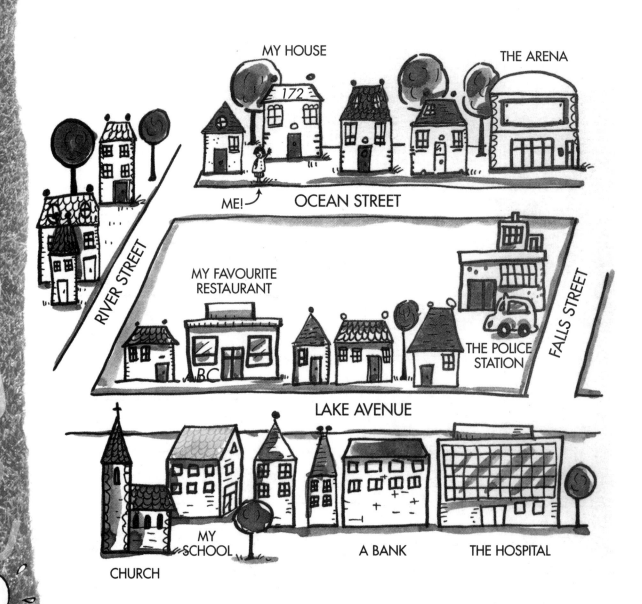

MY HOUSE

THE ARENA

172

ME!

OCEAN STREET

RIVER STREET

MY FAVOURITE RESTAURANT

THE POLICE STATION

FALLS STREET

BC

LAKE AVENUE

CHURCH

MY SCHOOL

A BANK

THE HOSPITAL

Junk food for Halloween!

Draw

Chips ____

Bubble gum ____
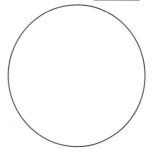

Peanuts ____

Jelly Beans ____

Chocolate ____
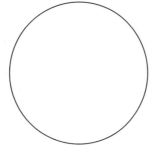

Caramel ____
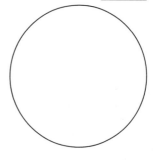

Gummy Bears ____
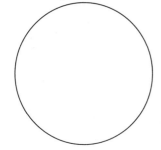

Popcorn ____
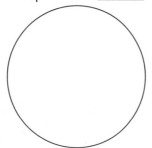

Candies ____
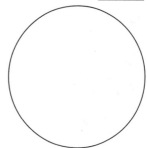

Put one ♡ = like

Put two ♡ ♡ = like a lot

Put three ♡ ♡ ♡ = love

example:
pizza ♡ ♡ ____

Where?

Question = Where?	Answer = (réponse) A place

Question:
Where is the spider?

Answer:
The spider is **on** the jack-o'-lantern.

To indicate a place, we use "prepositions".
Here are 4 prepositions: **On, in, in front of, next to.**

On	In
Q. Where is the spider?	Q. Where is the spider?

A. The spider is on the box.	A. The spider is in the box.
In front of	Next to
Q. Where is the spider?	Q. Where is the spider?

A. The spider is in front of the clown.	A. The spider is next to the clown.

Find the creatures

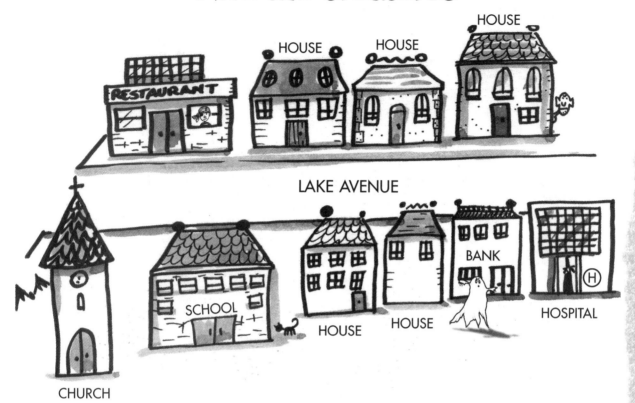

Halloween creatures are hiding on Lake Avenue.
Where? Write the preposition. Look at p. 62 for help.

1. Q. Where is the pirate?
   A. The pirate is **in** the **restaurant.**

2. Q. Where is the monster?
   A. The monster is _____ the _____ .

3. Q. Where is the witch?

   A. The witch is _____ the _____ .

4. Q. Where is the black cat?
   A. The black cat is _____ the _____ .

5. Q. Where is the ghost?
   A. The ghost is _____ the _____ .

My family

Meet Crocfun's family

Hi, let me
introduce my family!

Use Mister Alpha's code, p. 10

1. This is my _m o t h e r_.
Her name is Crocmom.

2. This is my _f a t h e r_.
His name is Crocdad.

3. This is my _b r o t h e r_.
His name is Crocbro.

4. This is my _s i s t e r_.
Her name is Crocsis.

66

This is my family

- My **MOTHER** is 36 years old. Her name is Crocmom. She likes (♡) music. Her favourite music is jazz.

- My **FATHER** is 35 years old. His name is Crocdad. He likes animals. His favourite animal is the lion.

- I have one **SISTER**. Her name is Crocsis. She is 11 years old and she likes sports. Her favourite sport is basketball.

- I have one **BROTHER**. His name is Crocbro. He is 7 years old. He likes hockey very much. His favourite hockey player is Wayne Gretzky.

- We have a domestic animal (a **PET**). It is a female cat. She is 1 year old. She likes to run and play with me. Her name is Grisou.

- My **BEST FRIEND**, Croque-Mots, is 8 years old and he likes to ski and play in the snow.

- And **ME**, Crocfun! I am 9 years old. I like pizza. It is my favourite food!

Looking for information

Read about Crocfun's family on page 67. Write the information.

Who (qui) ?	Name ?	Age ?	Favourite (♡)
Mother	crocmom	36	music jazz
father	Crocdad	35	lion
sister	Crocsis	11 years old	bascetball
Brother	Crocbro	7	Hockey Wayne Gretzky
Pet	Grisou	1	run and play
Best friend	croc-mats	8 years old	snow play
 ME!	Crocfun	9	food

I **love** pizza.
I **like** soccer **the best**.
I **like** Rap Music **very much**.
My favourite season is spring.

His or her?

* When we talk about a **girl**  or **woman**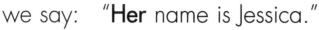
we say: "**Her** name is Jessica."
"**Her** favourite animal is a dog."

* When we talk about a **boy** or **man**
we say: "**His** name is Arthur."
"**His** favourite animal is a dog."

Write "his or her".

 1- Julie <u>Her</u> favourite animal is the giraffe.

2- Bob <u>His</u> favourite sport is baseball.

3- John <u>His</u> favourite animal is the snake.

4- Emilie <u>Her</u> address is 1234 Lake avenue.

5- <u>His</u> name is Jean-Sébastien.

6- <u>Her</u> name is Elizabeth.

Your family!

Tell me about your family. What is the name
of your mom, your dad... Write "his" or "her".

1- Mom: __ __ __ **name** is _____.
          His/Her

2- Dad: __ __ __ name is _____.

3- Brothers(s): __ __ __ name is _____.
                 __ __ __ ____ is _____.
                 __ __ __ ____ is _____.

No brothers? Check (✔) this box here => ☐

4- Sister(s): __ __ __ name is _____.
               __ __ __ ____ is _____.
               __ __ __ ____ is _____.

No sisters? Check here => ☐

5- Pet: "**His**" if your pet is a male
         "**Her**" if your pet is a female
                 __ __ __ **name** is _____.
                 His/Her

My pet is a _____.   No pets ? => ☐
              (Dog, cat...)

70

More about your family!

"DEMI-FRÈRE" is STEPBROTHER in English!
"DEMI-SOEUR" is STEPSISTER in English!

Do you have stepbrothers or stepsisters?
Write the names. Write "His or Her".

1- Stepbrother(s)

__ __ __ name is _____ .
His/Her

__ __ __ _____ is _____ .

2- Stepsister(s)

__ __ __ _____ is _____ .
His/Her

__ __ __ _____ is _____ .

Who (qui) are your best friends (amis)?

I have _____ best friends (1-2-3...?)

• __ __ __ name is _____ .
His/Her

• __ __ __ _____ is _____ .

• __ __ __ _____ is _____ .

• __ __ __ _____ is _____ .

Age

How old are you?

I am 8 years old

Catherine   Alexis

Practise… (Look at p. 67)

1. How old is Crocfun? He is _____ years old.
2. How old is Croque-Mots? He is _____ years old.
3. How old is Crocmom? She is _____ years old.
4. How old is Alexis? He is _____ years old.

And **you** ?

5. Q: H _ _ _ _ d _ r _ _ _ u ?

    A: I _ _ _____ y _ _ _ s _ _ d .
              (number)

Your Dad ?

6. Q: H _ _ _ _ _ is your dad?

    A: He _ s _____ y _ _ _ _ _ _ _ .
               (number)

Pronouns

 First (1ˢᵗ) person singular   JE   → I

 Second (2ⁿᵈ) person singular   TU   → YOU

 Third (3ʳᵈ) person singular   IL (A boy)   → HE

 ELLE (A girl)   → SHE

 (For an object) → IT

First person plural   Nous   → WE

 Second person plural   Vous   → YOU

Third person plural   ILS/ELLES   → THEY

Choose the right pronoun.

1. ___ am a crocodile.

4. ___ is a girl in my class.

2. ___ are good friends.

5. ___ is my new bicycle.

3. ___ likes to play football.

6. ___ are 10 years old.

How old?

WATCH OUT!
IN FRENCH, I SAY:
"Quel âge **as**-tu?"
[Verbe **Avoir**]

IN ENGLISH, I SAY:
"HOW OLD **ARE** YOU?"
[Verbe **Être**]

QUESTION   **Pronouns**   ANSWER

	QUESTION			ANSWER	
1st p.s.	How old **am**	I ?	I	**am**	7 years old.
2nd p.s.	How old **are** you ?		You	**are**	8 years old.
3rd p.s.	(Boy) How old **is**	he ?	He	**is**	9 years old.
	(Girl) How old **is**	she ?	She	**is**	12 years old.
	(object) How old **is**	it ?	It	**is**	13 years old.
1st p.p.	How old **are** we ?		We	**are**	15 years old.
2nd p.p.	How old **are** you ?		You	**are**	16 years old.
3rd p.p.	How old **are** they ?		They	**are**	17 years old.

This is the **verb** " TO BE " (être)
in English. Now you have to practise!

Be a detective...

Ask your family questions. Look at p. 74.

1. How old is your mother?
   She __is__ __49__ y e a r s o l d
   (pronoun) (verb to be) (number)

2. How old is your father?
   He __is__ __47__ 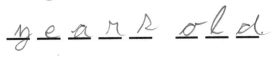 _years old_
   (pronoun) (to BE) (number)

3. How old ~~is~~ are your sister?
   ~~They~~ _are 15, 18, 20 years old._

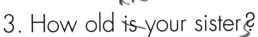
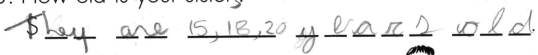

4. How old is your brother?
   H_ _ _ _ _ _ _ _ _ _ _ _ _

What about your family? – A survey

Complete this grid describing your Mom, Dad,
brothers (stepbrothers), sisters (stepsisters),
your friend, your pet... and YOU!

Who (qui)?	Name?	Age? (How old...?)	Favourite (♡)
Mother (MOM)			
Father (DAD)			
Pet			
ME!			

A family tree

Find 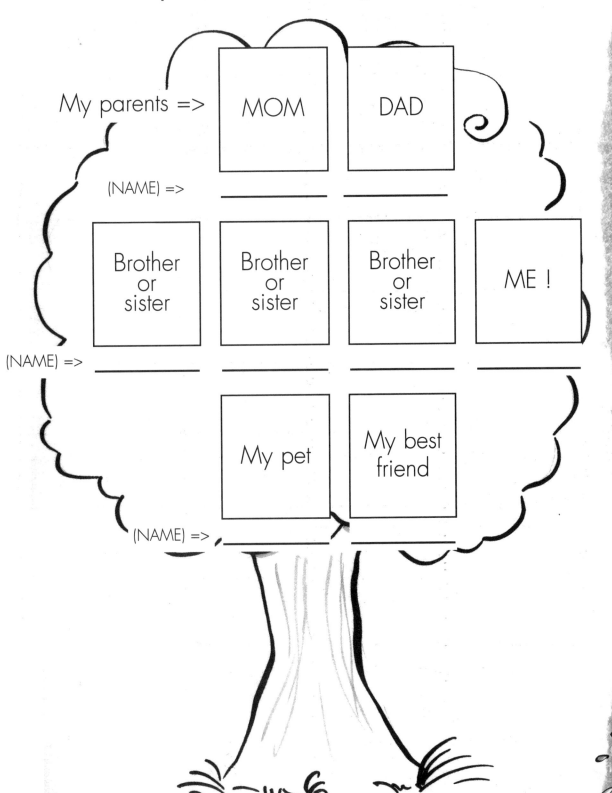 pictures of the members of your family.
Glue the pictures in the rectangles. Write the names.

My parents =>

| MOM | DAD |

(NAME) =>

_____

| Brother or sister | Brother or sister | Brother or sister | ME ! |

(NAME) =>

_____

| My pet | My best friend |

(NAME) => _____

77

Boy or girl ?

I am a girl.

I am a boy.

What about you?

I __ __ a _____ (boy, girl)
(verb to be)

Draw a picture of yourself.

Words, words, words
"description"

HAIR

Short hair

Long hair

Straight hair

Wavy hair

Curly hair

HAIR COLOUR

noir = Black hair

gris = Grey hair

blanc = White hair

blond = Blond hair

Brun = Brown hair

roux = Red hair

châtain = Chestnut brown hair

SIZE

Short

Average height

Tall

I (have) short, curly hair.

I (have) red hair.

I (have) blue eyes.

I (am) average height

Verb **Have** = **Avoir**

Verb **To be** = **Être**

(See "How Old?" p. 74)

79

Describe yourself

NAME: My name is _Arielle Anna Sloutsker_

AGE: I am _9_ years old.
number

HAIR: I have _straight_ hair.
(long, curly, straight…)

I have _dark blond_ hair.
(colour)

EYES: I have _blue_ eyes.
(colour)

SIZE: I am _average_.
(short…)

FAVOURITES: ♡ ♡

My favourite music ♫ is _____.
My favourite sport is _pear ball_.
My favourite T.V. show is _____.
My favourite game is _____.
My favourite colour is _purple_.
My favorite _____ is _____.
(?)

Where is "to be"?

- We use "to be" to describe your feelings.
    Ex: They (are) scared.

- We use "to be" to say your age.
    Ex: I (am) 9 years old.

- We use "to be" to describe yourself.
    Ex: Vincent (is) tall.

The verb "to BE" is not here. It's gone! Look at the subject, look at p. 74 ("How old?") and conjugate the verb "to BE".

Ex: Antoine ___is___ happy.

1- Catherine ___is___ in grade 5.
2- I ___am___ 8 years old.
3- Frédérique ___is___ short.
4- We ___are___ in the Josée's class.
5- They ___are___ in grade 3.
6- You ___are___ proud.
7- Audrey ___is___ very tall.
8- Nicolas ___is___ a good hockey player.
9- I ___am___ short and thin.
10- The monkeys ___are___ funny.
11- This duck ___is___ yellow and brown.

81

The Seasons

Four seasons

In Quebec, the year has four seasons.

Winter

Spring

Summer

Fall or Autumn

Help with days, months and seasons

Days	Jours
Sunday	dimanche
Monday	lundi
Tuesday	mardi
Wednesday	mercredi
Thursday	jeudi
Friday	vendredi
Saturday	samedi

Months	Mois
January	janvier
February	février
March	mars
April	avril
May	mai
June	juin
July	juillet
August	août
September	septembre
October	octobre
November	novembre
December	décembre

Seasons	Saisons
spring	printemps
summer	été
fall or autum	automne
winter	hiver

How do you know it's winter?

Winter arrives on December 21.

The period of the shortest day and

the longest night is called:

Use this special number code:

1	3	5	7	9	11	13	15	17	19	21	23	25
E	J	T	F	M	R	H	S	V	C	Z	O	G

2	4	6	8	10	12	14	16	18	20	22	24	26
U	N	A	Y	X	B	W	L	P	I	Q	D	K

1. ___ ___ ___ ___ ___ ___ ___ ___
    15 23 16 15   5 20 19   1

short : ⊢——⊣

long : ⊢————————⊣

> When you add "est" at the end of an adjective, you modify the meaning of the adjective.
>
> Short + "est" => shortest day = jour le plus court
>
> Long + "est" => longest night = nuit la plus longue

2. **On December 25, we celebrate**
    (use the code):

___ ___ ___ ___ ___ ___ ___ ___ ___
19 13 11 20 15   5   9   6 15

Let's play outside

In Quebec, during winter, you can do a lot of fun activities. Complete the names of the activities using the "key words".

1. Build a...

_ _ _ _ _ _ _ t

2. Make a...
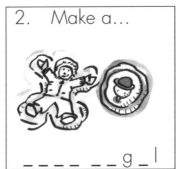
_ _ _ _ _ _ g _ l

3. Make a...

_ _ _ _ _ _ n

4. Go...

_ _ _ _ _ -
_ _ _ _ _ _ _ g

5. Go...

f _ _ _ _ _
_ _ _ _ _ _ g

6. Play...

_ _ c _ _ _

7. Go...

a _ _ _ _ _
s _ _ _ _ _

8. Go...

_ _ _ _ _ _ _ _

9. Go...

c _ _ _ _ -c _ _ _ _ _
s _ _ _ _ _

Word Bank

Sledding
Cross-country skiing
Snowboarding
Alpine skiing
Snowman

Figure skating
Snow angel
Hockey
Snow fort

Winter activities survey

Question:
"Do you like ♡ _____ skiing _____ ?"

Answer:
Yes, No, a little bit or I don't know (?)

A little bit = un peu.   I don't know = Je ne sais pas.

Find three persons, ask the questions, and check (✔) their answers.

Activities	name				name				name			
Answers	Yes	No	Little	(?)	Yes	No	Little	(?)	Yes	No	Little	(?)
Snowboarding												
Alpine skiing												
Sledding												
Hockey												
Figure skating												
Playing in the snow												
Snowshoeing												
Cross-country skiing												

What are the three most (+) popular activities ?

_____   _____   _____

Now, Your turn!

Answer the questions about your favourite winter activities.

Write complete answers.
Ex: Do you like playing in the snow?
    Choices:
- Yes, I do.
- No, I don't (negative = do + not = don't)
- Just a little bit (un peu)
- I don't know (je ne sais pas)

1. Do you like snowshoeing?

   _____

2. Do you like alpine skiing?

   _____

3. Do you like figure skating?

   _____

4. Do you like cross-country skiing?

   _____

5. Do you like snowboarding?

   _____

6. Do you like hockey?

   _____

7. Do you like sledding?

   _____

Animal tracks in the snow!

Crocfun and Crocbro are playing in the snow. They see different tracks in the snow.
Here are some animal tracks you can find in the snow in Quebec.

mouse tracks

squirrel tracks

crow tracks

rabbit tracks

cat tracks

Use your imagination and draw the tracks Crocfun leaves in the snow.

Dress up, it's cold !

On Halloween, you wear a costume.
In winter, you wear warm clothes.

Use "Mister Alpha's code" to find out about
winter clothes.

1.
___ ___ ___ ___ ___ ___

2.
___ ___ ___ ___ ___

3.
___ ___ ___ ___ ___ ___

4.
___ ___ ___ ___ ___ ___ ___

5.
___ ___ ___ ___ ___ ___ ___ ___

6.
___ ___ ___ ___ ___

___ ___ ___ ___ ___ ___

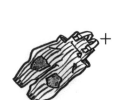 + = snowsuit

Mister Snowman

To build a nice snowman, you need branches ⟍⟋ , small rocks ● , a carrot 🥕 and... SNOW!

EARS · EYES · NOSE · MOUTH · NECK · HEAD · HAND · ARM · BODY · 1 FOOT · 2 FEET

On my hand, I have 5 fingers.

On my foot, I have 5 toes.

Oh where, oh where can it be ?

Crocfun lost his tuque . Help him find it.

Look at each snowman and choose the right preposition.
Remember

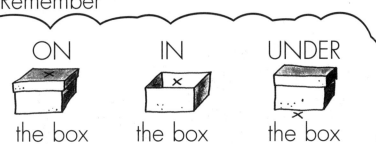

ON
the box

IN
the box

UNDER
the box

Help me!

1. Where is his tuque? It is _____ his head.

preposition

2. Where is his tuque? It ____ _____ his hand.

verb   preposition

3. W_____ is h__ _____ ?
   It _____ _____ his body.

verb   preposition

93

Don't forget

> Plural of verb to be = "are".
> Where (are) the mittens?

Now Crocfun has lost his mittens 🧤🧤. Help him.

1.  Where _a r e_ his mittens? They _a r e_ _under_ his body.

   (preposition)

2.  _Where a r e_ his _m i t t e n s_?
   They _a r e   on_ his nose .

   (preposition)

3.  Where _are_ his _mittens_?
   There   are   in his t_u g u e_.

   (verb)   (preposition)

Here are 2 snowmen. Draw boots 👢 and ask questions.
Write the answers.

Q _Where are the boots?_	
A _They are_ _on his hat_	
	.

Q _Where are the boots_ ?	
A _They are on his hands_	
	.

One season, three months !

In Quebec, winter lasts for three months.
Use the number code (p. 86)
and find the 3 months.

When you write months, always
use a capital letter at the beginning
Ex: <u>D</u>ecember   <u>S</u>eptember

1. $\overline{}\ \overline{}\ \overline{}\ \overline{}\ \overline{}\ \overline{}\ \overline{}\ \overline{}$
   24 1 19 1 9 12 1 11

2. $\overline{}\ \overline{}\ \overline{}\ \overline{}\ \overline{}\ \overline{}\ \overline{}$
   3 6 4 2 6 11 8

3. $\overline{}\ \overline{}\ \overline{}\ \overline{}\ \overline{}\ \overline{}\ \overline{}\ \overline{}$
   7 1 12 11 2 6 11 8

On December 25, we celebrate CHRISTMAS

On January 1, we celebrate NEW YEAR'S DAY

On February 14, we celebrate ST-VALENTINE'S day ♡

HAVE A GREAT WINTER

Word search

1. [J] [ ] [ ] [ ] [ ] [ ]

2. [ ] [ ] [C] [ ] [ ] [ ]

3. [ ] [T] - [ ] [ ] [ ] [ ] [ ] [ ] [ ] [E]

4. [ ] [O] [ ] [ ] [ ] [ ] [ ]

5. [ ] [ ] [ ] [ ] [ ] [T] [ ] [ ] [ ]

6. [ ] [ ] [Q] [ ] [ ]

7. [C] [ ] [ ] [ ] - [ ] [ ] [ ] [ ] [ ] [Y] [ ] [ ] [i] [i] [ ] [ ]

8. [R] [ ] [ ] [ ] [ ] [ ]

9. [ ] [ ] [ ] [W]

10. [C] [ ] [ ] [ ]

1. Month in winter

2. Mario Lemieux plays…

3. Feb 14th

4. Longest ☽ Shortest ☼

5. December 25th

6.

7. A winter sport with 3 words

8. Animal that loves carrots

9. tracks of a ✈

10. In winter it's __ __ __ __ (froid)

96

How do you know it's spring?

Spring arrives on March 21.
The period when the day and night are equal (=) in length has a special name.

Same length

SIGN CODE

Y	⌒	∥	♂	☒	△	○	◻	X	⤴	~	ↄ	ƒ
A	B	C	D	E	F	G	H	I	J	K	L	M

¥	☉	⚇	⚲	▷	✡	⊞	⟋	⊓	ᒥᒐ	✗	⊘	☉
N	O	P	Q	R	S	T	U	V	W	X	Y	Z

This period is called:
(use the sign code)

_ _ _ _ _ _ _ _ _ _

One season, three months part 2!

In Quebec, spring lasts for three months.

1. **Use the sign code to discover the 3 months**
   (use the sign code on p. 96).

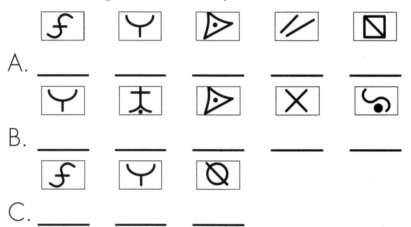

A. __ __ __ __ __

B. __ __ __ __ __

C. __ __ __

Don't forget your capital letters!

2. **Look at a calendar and answer the following questions.**

   A. How many days (jours) in March? _____ days
   B. How many days in April? _____ d _ _ _
   C. How many days in May? _____ _ _ _ _

 In spring we celebrate EASTER  Delicious!

In Quebec, spring just would not be spring without a visit to a sugar shack!

A Trip to the sugar shack!

Read the text.

Crocfun and his family decide to drive to the country. Crocuncle lives in a small village.

He has a farm. On his farm there is a forest of maple trees.

| ✡ | ☦ | ▷ | ✕ | ♀ | ○ |

Every __ __ __ __ __ Crocuncle produces maple syrup.

AFTER READING

Look at the question words "Who" "Where" "What" and complete the chart.

Who are the characters in the story:	Where are they going: Check ☑	What do they see !
1. _____	☐ city	
2. _____	☐ country	
3. _____	☐ mountain	_____
4. _____	☐ beach	_____
5. _____	☐ farm	_____
6. _____	☐ arena	_____
	☐ restaurant	_____
	☐ hospital	_____
	☐ sugar shack	_____
	☐ snack bar	

The sugar shack

Identify these objects.
Write the number in the correct circle.

1. sugar shack
2. evaporation house
3. barrel
4. spout
5. bucket

6. maple tree
7. window
8. door
9. horse
10. chimney

Sugar bush rally

Did you know that you install only 3 buckets per maple tree.
1 at the top   1 at the center   1 at the bottom.

Crocfun and Crocbro are helping Crocuncle collect the maple sap.

Look at the forest   . Read the instructions.

Write F when it's Crocfun's bucket **F**.
Write B when it's Crocbro's bucket **B**.

- Crocfun goes to tree A   and takes the center bucket. After, he goes to tree C   to collect sap in the top bucket. At the end, he takes the bottom bucket on tree D.

- Crocbro goes to tree E and takes the top and bottom buckets. Then, he goes to tree B to collect the sap in the center bucket.

We have sap from 6 buckets.
Now let's go to the sugar shack to make maple syrup!

Maple syrup

First step: Collect the sap (water from the maple).

Second step: Boil  the sap. It must be 104° Celsius. That's very hot!

Third step: Check and adjust the cooking temperature 104° C.

Fourth step: Filter the syrup.

Fifth step: Put the syrup in cans . That's it. Very simple!

Crocuncle! How many litres of sap do you need to make 1 litre of maple syrup?

To produce 1 litre of syrup, you must boil about 40 litres of sap.

Solving problems

> How many = combien

To make 1 litre of maple syrup, you need
(use the sign code on p. 97).

_____ _____ _____ _____ _____ litres of sap.

Problems:

1. Crocuncle wants to produce three cans
   of 1 litre each of maple syrup.
   How many litres of sap does he need?

   Answer

2. **How many** buckets of sap do you see on page
   100? _____

3. Crocmom wants cans of maple syrup.
   Each can is $3.00. She has $27.00.
   How many cans will she have ?

   Answer

How do you know it's summer?

Summer in Quebec arrives on June 21.
The period of the longest day and the shortest
night is called (use Mister Alpha's code, p. 10).

1. __ __ __ __ __ __ __ __ __ __ __ __

Find the page where you have learned this same word.

2. What page is it on? _____.

3. What season was it about? _____.

What's the difference between the Winter solstice and
the Summer solstice ?

Choose **longest** or **shortest**.

4.

Winter solstice		Summer solstice	

Let's get wet

Summer is great for water sports.

Complete the names of the activities using
the correct verbs in the word bank.

1.
to…

_ _ _ _

2.
to…

_ _ _ h

3.
to…

_ w _ _ _

4.
to…

_ i _ _ _

5.
to…

_ _ y _ _ _

6.
to…

_ _ o _ -
_ _ _

7.
to…

_ _ _ _ _ -
s _ _ _

8.
to…

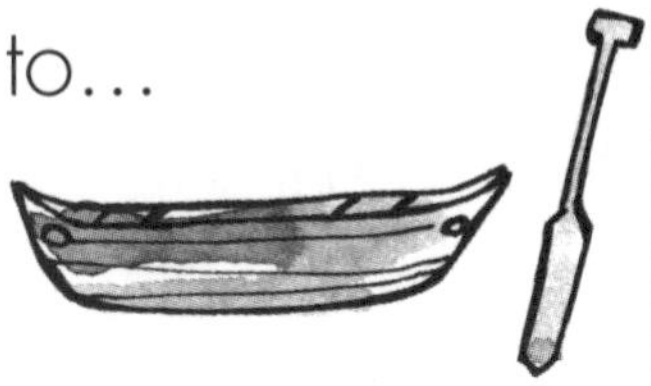

_ _ _ _ _

9.
to…

_ _ _ _
in the water

swim   canoe   kayak
snorkel   sail   fish
play   dive   windsurf

word
bank

I see land!

What about these activities.

1. To _ i _ _ _

a bicycle

2. To _ _ y
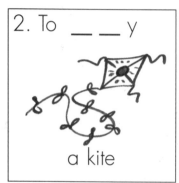
a kite

3. To p _ _ _

tennis

4. To ride

a _ _ r _ _

5. To

s _ _ _ _ _ -
_ _ _ _ d

6. To
_ _ _ _ _

a tree

7. To _ _ _ _ _
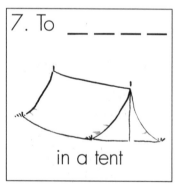
in a tent

8. To
_ _ _ -
_ _ _ _ _

skate

9. To
_ _ _ _ _ _

Word Bank

ride	climb	play
skateboard	camp	horse
fly	garden	in-line

106

Fly me to the ... ?

Hey, Croque-Mots. Do you have a kite?

What does it look like?

Wow! Can I see it?

Yes. It is beautiful!

It has a dragon, 2 suns and one star.

Yes. Look.

Do you have a kite?
Draw your kite here.

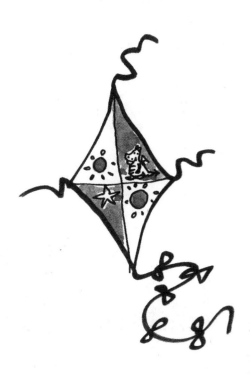

Conjugate to have

In English, you conjugate the verb to have (avoir) this way.

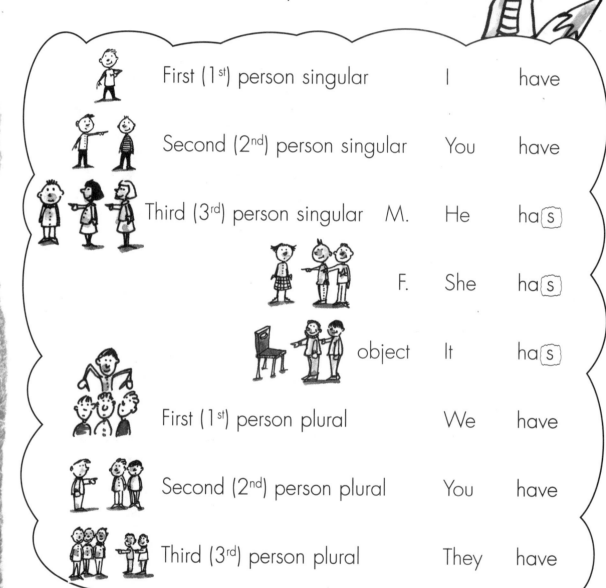

	First (1st) person singular		I	have
	Second (2nd) person singular		You	have
	Third (3rd) person singular	M.	He	ha(s)
		F.	She	ha(s)
		object	It	ha(s)
	First (1st) person plural		We	have
	Second (2nd) person plural		You	have
	Third (3rd) person plural		They	have

Conjugate "to have" correctly.

1. I _have_ a ball.
2. You _have_ a skateboard.
3. She _has_ a C.D.
4. He _has_ a dog.

5. It _has_ 4 legs (the chair).
6. We _have_ permission.
7. You _have_ the solution.
8. They _have_ a big garden.

108

Do you have _____ ?

Question:
Do you have a dog? < Answer
Yes, I have a dog.
No, I do not have a dog.

Check "yes" or "no" and complete the answer.
Check ☑

1. Do you have a bicycle? ☑Yes ☐No I _have a bike_.

2. Do you have a tent? ☑Yes ☐No _I have a tent._

3. Do you have a skateboard? ☐Yes ☑No _I don't have a skateboard_

4. Do you have a brother? ☐Yes ☑No _I don't have a brother._

5. Do you have a sister? ☑Yes ☐No _I have three sisters_

(How many – Let's review.)

1. How many wheels 🚲 does a bicycle have?
It _has two wheels_.

2. How many triangles does the sailboat ⛵ have?
It _has two triangles._

3. How many legs 🐴 does a horse have?
It has four legs.

109

Undress, it's hot

In winter, you wear **warm** clothes.
In summer, you wear **light** clothes.

Use the sign code on p. 97

1.  t - s h i r t

2.  s h o r t s

3. d r e s s   4.  s k i r t

5. h a t

6.  s w e a t s h i r t

7.  r u n n i n g   s h o e s

8. p a n t s

9. c a p

10. s w i m s u i t

11. s w e a t e r

Clothing

Write 2 pieces of clothing you wear and draw them.

Example: What do you wear when you play baseball?

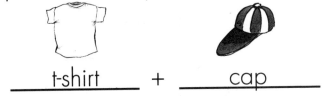

___t-shirt___   +   ___cap___

What do you wear:

1. When you play tennis?   _____   _____

2. When you skateboard?   _____   _____

3. When you garden?   _____   _____

4. When you in-line skate?   _____   _____

5. When you camp?   _____   _____

Action words = verbs

Draw the following action words (see p. 105-106).

To ride a bicycle

To sail

To fly a kite

To swim

To fish

To climb

When you put "to" in front of a verb,
it is the infinitive form.
Ex: jouer – to play –

Present tense

In the present tense, most verbs take "s"
only in the third person singular.

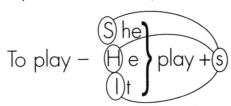

To play –
{ (S)he, (H)e, (I)t } play + (s)

Complete the charts by using the correct ending.

Example: **Your turn**

1. TO PLAY

I	play
You	play
(S)he (H)e (I)t }	play (s)
We	play
You	play
They	play

2. TO RIDE

I	*ride*
You	*ride*
(S)he (H)e (I)t }	*rides*
We	*ride*
You	*ride*
They	*ride*

3. TO CLIMB

I	*climb*
you	*climb*
(S)he He It }	*climbs*
We	*climb*
You	*climb*
They	*climb*

4. TO SWIM

I	*swim*
You	*swim*
She He It }	*swim*
We	*swim*
You	*swim*
They	*swim*

5. TO DIVE

I	*dive*
You	*dive*
She He It }	*dives*
We	*dive*
You	*dive*
They	*dives*

6. TO SKATE

I	*skate*
You	*skate*
She He It }	*skates*
We	*skate*
You	*skate*
They	*skate*

One season, three months part 3!

In Quebec, summer lasts for three months

Can you guess the three months?

(Use the number code on p. 86)

1. __ __ __ __
    3   2   4   1

2. __ __ __ __
    3   2   16   8

Capital letter at the beginning

3. __ __ __ __ __ __
    6   2   25   2   15   5

4. In our province, we celebrate an important day on June 24.
What is it: _____.

5. In Canada, we celebrate an important day on July 1.
What is it: _____.

Draw these flags

QUEBEC (province)

CANADA (country)

114

How do you know it's fall?

Fall arrives on September 21. Like spring, fall begins when the day ☺ and the night ☾ are equal (=) in length. Do you remember the name of this special day?

It is called the __ __ __ __ __ __ __
(go to page 97 for the answer!)

In Quebec fall is famous for the beautiful colours in trees. FALL also means "tomber". During FALL (the season), the leaves FALL (the verb "tomber")!

The leaves of the trees FALL.
It must be FALL!

We can also name this season Autumn. Autumn or Fall.

115

Rake them up

A RAKE / TO RAKE THE LEAVES

Crocfun loves ♥♥♥ to rake the leaves. Who (a person) is going to help Crocfun? Follow the leaves to find the answer!

Croque-Mots

Crocmom

Crocbro

Crocdad

START

ANSWER: _____

will help Crocfun!

You are the apple of my eye

In Quebec, apples are ready during fall.
Some apples are named Lobo, others are McIntosh,
others are Spartan. Some apples are big,
others are small. Some apples are RED,
some are GREEN, and others are YELLOW.

Put colour
in the colours! Colour
the colours!

Some apples are SWEET
(chocolate is **sweet**) and others are
SOUR (a yellow lemon is **sour**).

But all apples are DELICIOUS!

Doctor Croc says…

"An apple a day
keeps the doctor away!
Apples are good for you!
Eat apples!"

Apple lover

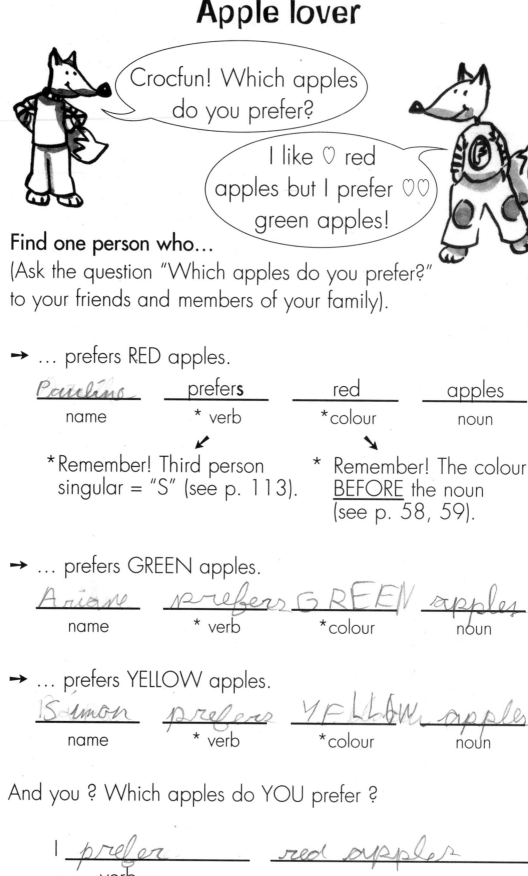

Crocfun! Which apples do you prefer?

I like ♡ red apples but I prefer ♡♡ green apples!

Find one person who...
(Ask the question "Which apples do you prefer?" to your friends and members of your family).

→ ... prefers RED apples.

Pauline	prefer**s**	red	apples
name	* verb	*colour	noun

↘ *Remember! Third person singular = "S" (see p. 113).

↘ * Remember! The colour <u>BEFORE</u> the noun (see p. 58, 59).

→ ... prefers GREEN apples.

Ariane	_prefers_	_GREEN_	_apples_
name	* verb	*colour	noun

→ ... prefers YELLOW apples.

Simon	_prefers_	_YELLOW_	_apples_
name	* verb	*colour	noun

And you ? Which apples do YOU prefer ?

I	_prefer_		_red apples_
	verb		

No "S"! It's 1st person singular!

Pick me up!

September, the ninth month of the year, is the perfect month to **pick** apples.

**How many apples can Crocfun pick in each tree?
Spell the numbers.**

Tree 1 =

1. _ _ _ _ _ _ _ apples

Tree 2 =

2. _ _ _ _ _ _ _ _ apples

Tree 3 =

3. _ _ _ _ _ apples

Tree 4 =

4. _ _ _ _ _ _ _ _ apples

Good things with apples...
Draw ✗, ♡ or ♡♡

Apple **juice**

Apple **sauce** (compote)

An apple **turnover**

Apple **jelly**

An apple **pie**

119

Indoor fun

During fall, sometimes the temperature is not very nice. Sometimes it rains . Crocfun likes to play in the leaves but on a rainy day, he also likes to do activities inside his house .

Complete the activities. Use the word bank.

2. Play _ _ _ _ s

1. _ a _ _ _ TV

4. _ _ _ _

3. Play on a _ o _ _ _ _ _ _

5. Play _ h _ _ _

6. _ _ _ _ _ _ _ t stamps or hockey cards

7. L _ _ _ _ _ _ to music

Word Bank

draw   cards   listen

collect   watch   chess

build   computer

8. _ _ i _ _ a model

120

A week in Crocfun's life

NOVEMBER

Su	Mo	Tu	We	Th	Fr	Sa
					3	4
5	6	7	8	9		

On **Fr**iday, November 3, it is my friend Croque-Mots' birthday. We will play cards and eat popcorn! On **Sa**turday, November 4, I will build my new model. On **Su**nday, I will play chess with my brother after lunch. I will watch my favourite TV program on **Mo**nday, November 6 and on **Th**ursday the 9th. On **Tu**esday, November 7, I will play cards with Crocsis and my mom. Finally, on **We**dnesday the 8th, I will draw in my colouring book with my father.

Read and complete.

DAYS (jours)	ACTIVITY	WITH (avec)
Fr		
Sa		✕
Su		
Mo		✕
Tu		
We		
Th		✕

Days, days, days!

Look at the calendar. The first (1ˢᵗ) day of the week
(on the left ←) is S u _ _ _ _.

Write the 5 days of school in order.

1. M o _ _ _ _
2. T u _ _ _ _ _
3. W e _ _ _ _ _ _ _
4. T h _ _ _ _ _ _
5. F r _ _ _ _

Write the 2 days of the weekend.

6. S a _ _ _ _ _ _
7. S u _ _ _ _

Like months, days of
the week begin with a
CAPITAL letter!

What is your favourite day of the week?
I like _____.

My agenda

Write the days of the week.
Write the activities you do every day of this week.
If you're not alone (seul), write the name of the person with you.

DAY	ACTIVITY	WITH (avec)?
S u _ _ _ _		
M _ _ _ _ _		
T _ _ _ _ _ _		
W _ _ _ _ _ _ _ _		
T _ _ _ _ _ _ _		
F _ _ _ _ _		
S _ _ _ _ _ _ _		

One season, three months part 4!

In Quebec, fall or autumn lasts for three months.

Can you guess the three months?

1. __ __ __ __ __ __ __ __ __ __

2. __ __ __ __ __ __ __ __ __

3. __ __ __ __ __ __ __ __ __ __ __

SPECIAL HOLIDAYS

4. On October 31, wear a costume and watch out for bats and witches. It's H _ l _ _ w _ _ _.

5. On October _____, we celebrate THANKSGIVING (Action de Grâce).

On November 25, we celebrate ST-CATHERINE'S DAY.

Let's review months!

Can you write the 12 months again?
If you need help, look at p. 85.

1. A. J _ _ _ _ _ _   G. _ _ _ _
   B. _ _ _ _ _ _ _ _   H. _ _ _ _ _ _
   C. _ _ _ _ _   I. _ _ _ _ _ _ _ _ _
   D. _ _ _ _ _   J. _ _ _ _ _ _ _
   E. _ _ _   K. _ _ _ _ _ _ _ _
   F. _ _ _ _   L. D _ _ _ _ _ _ _

2. Don't forget the CAPITAL letters at the beginning!

   A. What is your favourite month?
      _____.

   B. During which month do you celebrate your birthday?
      _____.

   C. When is St-Valentine's day?
      In _____.

   D. When is the first day of school?
      _____.

   E. When is the summer solstice?
      _____.

   F. When is New Year's day?
      _____.

Christmas

Christmas

Christmas is December 25. It is during a season called winter. Many children love ♡♡ Christmas because they have a big **party** with mom and dad, brothers and sisters, grandparents, uncles, aunts and cousins. Everybody is happy. Young children put **milk** and **cookies** in the **living room** for SANTA CLAUS.

Some people give and receive cards and gifts.

Some people decorate their house and a Christmas tree.

MERRY CHRISTMAS!

Christmas fun

Use your coloured pencils to colour this!

Make a Christmas card

1. Choose a nice sheet of paper (white, red or green).

2. Fold it in two.

3. Fold it in two, again!

4. On the front of the card, draw a big Santa Claus or a Reindeer or a Christmas tree or an angel or…

5. Open the card.

6. Inside the card, write "MERRY CHRISTMAS". Write big colourful letters. Draw pictures. Decorate the inside. Use colours! Use your imagination! Have fun!

7. Give the card to someone you ♡!

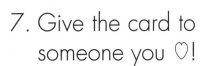

A-maze-ing Santa

1. Help Santa find his elves…
2. Help Rudolf find the sleigh…
3. Help Crocfun find a Christmas tree…

A sleigh ride

Read the story and write numbers 2 to 10 in the correct circles to indicate the order of Rudolf's stops.
Look at p. 60 for help.

Rudolf is visiting the city to say "HELLO" to his friends. His 1st stop is at the hospital. Then he goes to Tim's house. His address is 164 Elf street. Stop #3 is at the church. Then Rudolf goes to the store on Angel Avenue. Next, he goes to the restaurant for a good sandwich. Stop #6 is at the park to play. After, he goes to the gas station and the book store. Rudolf then goes to Rachel's house. Her address is 54 Rednose Road. Finally, stop #10 is at school to see the children.

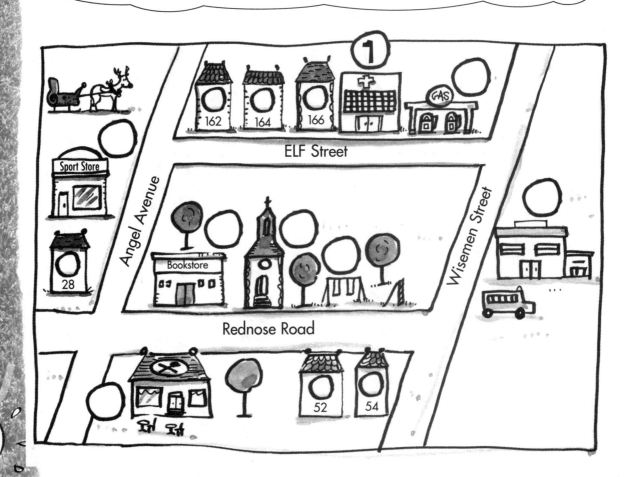

Describing gifts

BIG and small

Tall and short

Long

A BOW

RIBBON

Paper with polka dots

Paper with lines or stripes

Draw a BIG, TALL gift with blue paper, white LINES, a SMALL BOW, brown RIBBON and orange DOTS...

From me to you...

Match the card and the gift to the right person.

TO: CROCMOM
A short gift with blue paper and yellow stars.
FROM: CROCFUN

CARD A

TO: CROCBRO
A long gift with red paper and a simple bow.
FROM: CROCFUN

CARD B

TO: CROCDAD
A small and round gift with yellow paper and green polka dots and a blue bow.
FROM: CROCFUN

CARD D

TO: CROCSIS
A big gift with pink paper, red strips and white bow.
FROM: CROCFUN

CARD C

gift 1

gift 2

gift 3

gift 4

card	gift		card	gift		card	gift		card	gift

FATHER

BROTHER

SISTER

MOTHER

Now you can colour the gifts. Read the cards again.

Solutions

page 10

A apple	**B** boy	**C** cake	**D** duck	**E** egg	**F** fish
G girl	**H** hockey	**I** ice cream	**J** juice	**K** kite	**L** lemon
M monkey	**N** nose	**O** owl	**P** pencil	**Q** queen	**R** rainbow
S sun	**T** tulip	**U** unicorn	**V** vacuum	**W** web	**X** xylophone
Y yogurt	**Z** zipper				

page 11

Letters   Pictures

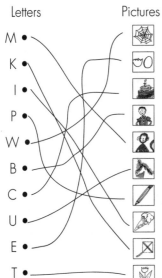

M •
K •
I •
P •
W •
B •
C •
U •
E •
T •

page 12

1. A. fish;
   B. hockey;
   C. sun;
   D. owl;
   E. girl;
   F. duck;
   G. queen;
   H cake;
   I. apple;
   J. yogurt;

2. Charles plays the xylophone.

135

Solutions

page 13

English is super!

page 14

1. The monkey and the owl have funny eyes.
2. The tulip is pink.
3. The girl and the boy play hockey.
4. The sun and the lemon are yellow.
5. The queen eats ice cream.

page 18

2. nine; 3. seven; 4. twelve; 5. ten;
6. eight; 7. four; 8. eleven; 9. three;
10. two; 11. five; 12. six.

page 19

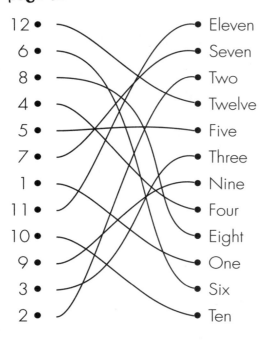

page 20

1. twelve;
2. six;
3. ten;
4. eight;
5. seven;
6. eleven;
7. five;
8. four;
9. nine;
10. one.

page 21

2. twelve;
3. nine;
4. four;
5. eight;
6. eleven;
7. eleven;
8. twelve;
9. ten;
10. nine;
11. ten;
12. ten.

page 22

2. six kites;
3. one queen;
4. two girls;
5. one tulip;
6. four pencils.

page 23

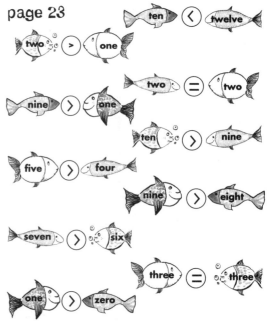

Solutions

page 24

1. two x two = four
2. <u>zero</u> x nine = zero
3. 1 🥚0 x 5 🥚0 = <u>five</u> eggs
4. one x one = <u>one</u>
5. <u>two</u> x four = 8
6. 5 🌷 x <u>ten</u> 🌷 = ten <u>tu</u>lips
7. one x <u>two</u> = two
8. <u>seven</u> x one = 7
9. three ☀ x 2 ☀ = <u>six</u> <u>su</u>ns
10. three x two = <u>six</u>
11. one x eleven = <u>eleven</u>
12. eleven ✕ x one ✕ = 11 <u>kite</u>s
13. four x one = <u>four</u>
14. four x <u>two</u> = eight
15. six x tw<u>o</u> = tw<u>elve</u>
16. five x two = <u>ten</u>
17. two x <u>five</u> = ten
18. one 🍋 x 0 🍋 = <u>zero</u> <u>le</u>mons
19. two x <u>three</u> = six
20. zero x e<u>l</u>even = <u>zero</u>

page 25

		s	i	**x**			
			e				
			v				
			e				
		t	e	n			
	t	**w**	o				
		e					
e	l	e	v	**e**	n	f	o	u	**r**
o		v		i		i	
n	i	n	e		g		v	
e				t	h	r	e	e
				t			

page 27

1. four;
2. seventeen;
3. six, seven;
4. nineteen;
5. eight;
6. eighteen;
7. nine, seven;
8. fourteen, sixteen;
9. four, three, two;
10. thirteen, seventeen.

page 28

2. I see <u>five</u> tulips.
3. I see <u>two</u> girls.
4. I see <u>two</u> cakes.
5. I see <u>one</u> owl.
6. I see <u>fourteen</u> eggs.
7. I see <u>five</u> noses.
8. I see <u>five</u> pencils.
9. I see <u>three</u> boys.
10. I see <u>sixteen</u> lemons.
11. I see <u>three</u> kites.
12. I see <u>one</u> fish.
13. I see <u>four</u> xylophones.
14. I see <u>one</u> rainbow.

page 29

1. one; 2. two;
3. three; 4. four;
5. five; 6. six;
7. seven; 8. eight;
9. nine; 10. ten;
11. eleven; 12. twelve;
13. thirteen; 14. fourteen;
15. fifteen; 16. sixteen;
17. seventeen; 18. eighteen;
19. nineteen; 20. twenty.

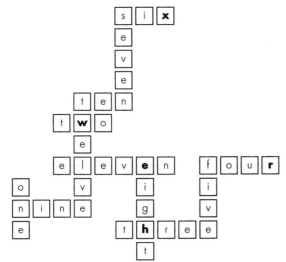

page 32
1. no; 2. yes;
3. yes; 4. yes;
5. no; 6. yes;
7. no; 8. no;
9. yes; 10. yes.

page 34
1. grey; 2. red;
3. blue; 4. white;
5. purple; 6. green;
7. yellow; 8. pink;
9. brown; 10. black.

page 35
1. yellow; 2. red; 3. brown; 4. white;
5. red, blue, yellow, orange, purple
and green.

page 38
1. circle;
2. rectangle;
3. square, triangle;
4. square, rectangle, circles;
5. triangles, ovals, rectangles.

page 41
A. 12 squares;
B. 4 grey rectangles
C. 5 grey circles;
D. 3 grey triangles
E. 3 stars;
F. 1 heart;
G. 16 white rectangles;
H. 7 white circles;
I. 20 white triangles

page 42
We love colours.

page 46
1. Good afternoon;
2. Good night!;
3. Good morning! How are you?
   Good morning! I am fine;
4. Good evening! What's your name?
   Good evening! My name is Crocfun!

page 50
1. I (ghost);
2. E (cat);
3. C (clown);
4. L (monster);
5. G (skeleton);
6. H (fairy);
7. D (pirate);
8. M (ballerina);
9. A (witch);
10. K (vampire);
11. F (spider);
12. B (bat);
13. J (scarecrow).

page 51
1. ghost;
2. graveyard;
3. witch;
4. clown;
5. cat;
6. scarecrow.

page 52

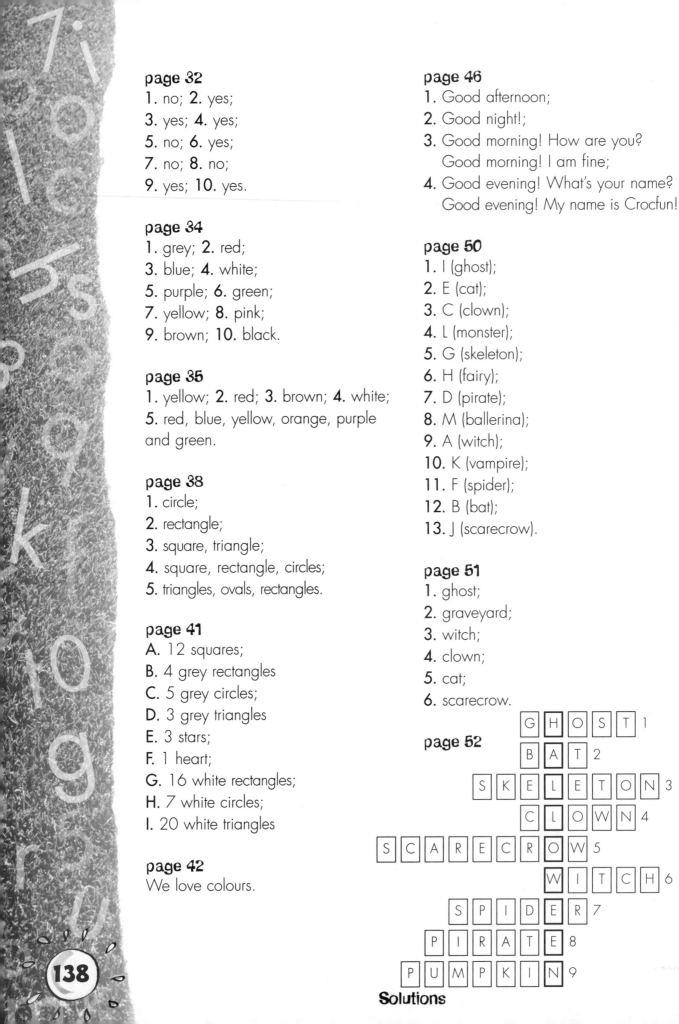

138

page 54
1. Two; 2. Four.

page 59
B. black bat;

C. white ghosts;

D. red nose.

1. one purple hat;

2. a white skeleton;

3. a brown cat;

4. a pink ballerina;

5. two black and white pirates;

6. eight black spiders;

7. three brown scarecrows;

8. one green monster.

page 63
2. The monster is **next to** the **house**;

3. The witch is **in the hospital**;

4. The black cat is **next to** the **school**;

5. The ghost is **in front** of the **bank**.

page 66
1. mother; 2.father; 3. brother; 4. sister.

page 69
1. **Her** favourite animal is the giraffe;

2. **His** favourite sport is baseball;

3. **His** favourite animal is the snake;

4. **Her** address is 1234 Lake Avenue;

5. **His** name is Jean-Sébastien;

6. **Her** name is Elizabeth

page 72
1. 9; 2. 8; 3. 36; 4. 8;

5. How old are you? I am ___ years old;

6. How old, he is ___ years old.

page 73
1. I;

2. we

3. he

4. she;

5. it;

6. you/they.

page 75
1. is __ years old;

2. is __ years old;

3. She is __ years old;

4. He is __ years old.

page 78
I am a boy or I am a girl.

page 81
1. Catherine **is** in grade 5;

2. I **am** 8 years old;

3. Frédérique **is** short;

4. We **are** in Josée's class;

5. They **are** in grade 3;

6. You **are** proud;

7. Audrey **is** very tall;

8. Nicolas **is** a good hockey player;

9. I **am** short and thin;

10. The monkeys **are** funny;

11. This duck **is** yellow and brown.

page 68

WHO (qui) ?	NAME ?	AGE ?	FAVOURITE ♥
Mother	Crocmom	36 years old	jazz
Father	Crocdad	35 years old	lion
Sister	Crocsis	11 years old	basketball
Brother	Crocbro	7 years old	Hockey Wayne Gretzky
Pet	Grisou	1 year old	Run and play with me
Best friend	Croque-Mots	8 years old	Play in the snow and ski
ME!	Crocfun	9 years old	pizza

Solutions

page 86
1. solstice;
2. Christmas

page 87
1. snow fort;
2. snow angel;
3. snowman;
4. snowboarding;
5. figure skating;
6. hockey;
7. alpine skiing;
8. sledding;
9. cross-country skiing;

page 91
1. a tuque;
2. boots;
3. a scarf;
4. mittens;
5. snowpants;
6. a snow jacket.

page 93
1. It is <u>on</u> the head;
2. It is <u>in</u> the hand;
3. **Where** is **his tuque?** It is <u>under</u> his body.

page 94
1. Where **are** his mittens? They **are under** his body;
2. Where **are** his **mittens?** They **are** on his nose;
3. Where **are** his mittens? **They are in** his tuque.

page 95
1. December;
2. January;
3. February.

page 96
1. JANUARY
2. HOCKEY
3. ST - VALENTINE
4. SOLSTICE
5. CHRISTMAS
6. TUQUE
7. CROSS COUNTRY SKIING
8. RABBIT
9. CROW
10. COLD

page 97
EQUINOX

page 98
1. A. March;   B. April;   C. May;
2. A. 31;   B. 30 days;   C. 31 days.

page 99
Spring

Who are the characters in the story:	Where are they going: Check ☑	What do they see 👁 👁 !
1. Crocfun	☐ city	farm
2. Crocbro	☑ country	village
3. Crocsis	☐ mountain	forest
4. Crocmom	☐ beach	maple
5. Crocdad	☑ farm	trees
6. Crocuncle	☐ arena	_____
	☐ restaurant	
	☐ hospital	
	☑ sugar shack	
	☐ snack bar	

page 100

140

Solutions

page 101

page 103
forty
1. 120;
2. 7;
3. 9 cans.

page 104
1. solstice;
2. p. 86;
3. winter
4.

Winter solstice		Summer solstice	
🌙	☀️	🌙	☀️
longest	shortest	shortest	longest

page 105
1. sail;
2. fish;
3. swim;
4. dive;
5. kayak;
6. snorkel;
7. windsurf;
8. canoe;
9. play in the water.

page 106
1. To ride a bicycle;
2. To fly a kite;
3. To play tennis;
4. To ride a horse;
5. To skateboard;
6. To climb a tree;
7. To camp in a tent;
8. To in-line skate;
9. To garden.

141

Solutions

page 108

1. I **have** a ball;
2. You **have** a skateboard;
3. She **has** a C.D.;
4. He **has** a dog;
5. It **has** 4 legs;
6. We **have** permission;
7. You **have** the solution;
8. They **have** a big garden.

page 109

1. It **has** two wheels;
2. It **has** three triangles;
3. It **has** four legs.

page 110

1. t-shirt;
2. shorts;
3. dress;
4. skirt;
5. hat;
6. sweatshirt ;
7. running shoes;
8. pants;
9. cap;
10. swimsuit;
11. sweater.

page 113

1. I ride, you ride, she rides, he rides, it rides, we ride, you ride, they ride.
2. I climb, you climb, she climbs, he climbs, it climbs, we climb, you climb, they climb.
3. I swim, you swim, she swims, he swims, it swims, we swim, you swim, they swim.
4. I dive, you dive, she dives, he dives, it dives, we dive, you dive, they dive.
5. I skate, you skate, she skates, he skates, skates, we skate, you skate, they skate.

page 114

1. June;
2. July;
3. August;
4. Saint-Jean Baptiste ou Fête nationale;
5. Canada Day.

page 115

Equinox

page 116

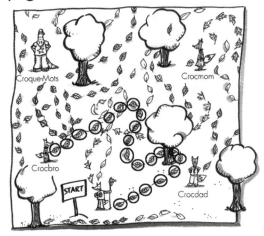

Crocbro

page 119

1. twelve;
2. fifteen;
3. nine;
4. eighteen.

page 120

1. watch;
2. cards;
3. computer;
4. draw;
5. chess;
6. collect;
7. listen;
8. build.

Solutions

page 121

DAYS (jours)	ACTIVITY	WITH (avec)
Friday	play cards and eat popcorn	Croque-Mots
Saturday	build model	✕
Sunday	play chess	My brother
Monday	watch TV	✕
Tuesday	play cards	Crocsis and my mom
Wednesday	draw	My father
Thursday	watch TV	✕

page 122
Sunday

1. Monday;
2. Tuesday;
3. Wednesday;
4. Thursday;
5. Friday;
6. Saturday;
7. Sunday.

page 124
1. September;
2. October;
3. November;
4. Halloween;
5. La réponse varie selon l'année.

page 128
1. A. January;
   B. February;
   C. March;
   D. April;
   E. May;
   F. June;
   G. July;
   H. August;
   I. September;
   J. October;
   K. November;
   L. December.

2. C. February 14;
   D. La réponse varie selon l'année;
   E. June 21;
   F. January 1.

page 132

page 134

Card A: mother;
Card B: brother;
Card C: sister;
Card D: father.

Gift 1: sister;
Gift 2: mother;
Gift 3: brother;
Gift 4: father.

Solutions